ALASKA

A Photographic Journey

TEXT: **Stevens Dana Bunker**

CAPTIONS: **Fleur Robertson**

DESIGNED BY: **Teddy Hartshorn**

EDITORIAL: **Gill Waugh and Jane Adams**

PRODUCTION: **Ruth Arthur and David Proffit**

DIRECTOR OF PRODUCTION: **Gerald Hughes**

DIRECTOR OF PUBLISHING: **David Gibbon**

CLB 2446
©1990 Colour Library Books Ltd., Godalming, Surrey, England.
All rights reserved.
This 1996 edition is published by Crescent Books,
a division of Random House Value Publishing, Inc.,
40 Engelhard Avenue, Avenel, New Jersey 07001

Random House
New York • Toronto • London • Sydney • Auckland

Printed and bound in Malaysia.

ISBN 0 517 00178 0

14 13 12 11 10 9 8

ALASKA

A Photographic Journey

Text by
STEVENS DANA BUNKER

CRESCENT BOOKS
NEW YORK / AVENEL, NEW JERSEY

It was a warm spring morning in the waning days of the nineteenth century when my great-uncle George announced to the family that he was heading west to seek his fortune. Like thousands of other New Englanders he would follow the sun to see where it took him. Over fifty years later, he would reappear on the family doorstep with no more than he had taken with him other than stories of adventure and the memory of ... Alaska.

"The Great Land" to the north has attracted and fascinated people for thousands of years. Most who knew of the existence of this wild area would only ponder it from afar. Fortunately, in every race of people there are always a few hardy souls who are never satisfied with questions left unanswered. It is to these men and women that we owe our admiration for bringing us Alaska. But to think of Alaska as a frozen wilderness or our last frontier is to short-change ourselves and our 49th State. This mysterious and charismatic land is so much more than a stereotype. It is a complex mixture of cultures and opportunities, formed and leavened by history and legend. Alaska carries not only an image of pioneering individualism, but also a large part of the economic and social future of America. It is a legacy bequeathed to us by many diverse peoples.

While little is known about Alaska's first residents, it is believed they began crossing the now lost land bridge from Siberia between 15,000 and 40,000 years ago. These early settlers were probably hunters following game. They settled first on the mainland, eventually migrating inland and down the northern side of the Aleutian Islands and along Alaska's western coast to be close to the bountiful waters of the Bering Sea. They developed into skilled marine hunters and superb boatmen. These resourceful people wasted nothing as there was precious little to waste. Animal skin was turned into clothing, shelter and boats. Bone and rock became tools, weapons and art objects. Alaskan timber, such as the famous Sitka spruce to the south, and the more plentiful willow, provided heat and illumination. Skilled hands also turned the wood into masks, hats, paddles and harpoons.

The leaves of the alder tree were chewed to release the sap and rubbed on black fly and mosquito bites. Its bark was used for the preparation of red dyes. Spruce root was formed into snares and traps to catch birds and fish. The teeth of the wolf became fish hooks. Edible oils were produced from seals, fish and the forest loon.

These northern pioneers eventually developed into the three groups of early native peoples to inhabit Alaska; the Aleuts, the Eskimos, and the Indians.

The Aleuts, whose villages spread across the islands that bear their name, had a sophisticated maritime society centered on loosely structured communities. They were essentially an "Eskimoan" people whose unique culture had been shaped and changed by their island environment.

The Aleutian Islands were wet and windswept, although not quite as cold as the mainland interior. They were practically treeless, making Bering Sea driftwood a valuable commodity.

Polygamy was accepted as part of Aleut society so long as a man could fulfil his responsibilities. Slavery was common, and the slaves were individually owned, usually by the warrior who had captured them in combat.

The Aleuts, despite their apparent isolation, have always maintained contact with other cultures, and have both influenced, and borrowed from, early and modern neighbors. Indeed, the first major European contact with the native peoples of Alaska was with the Aleuts during the Russian expeditions of the eighteenth century.

Eskimos were, and still are, a culturally diverse people. At the time of the first Russian explorations, the Pacific Eskimos could be found from Kodiak Island over to Prince William Sound. The Bering Sea Eskimos, or Yupiks, represented the oldest of the

Eskimo cultures. To the far north lived the Inuit, or Arctic, Eskimos. By far the least numerous of the native peoples, and the most scattered due to the limited food resources, many of these northern dwellers have moved farther inland over the years. In spite of the image many people have, Alaskan Eskimos have never lived in igloos.

Eskimo villages were made up of shifting collections of families. Loyalties were owed to direct families and to the small social groups with whom the Eskimos lived and shared community dwellings. They hunted inland as well as on the coast. They were proficient whalers, and traded their bounty with other villages. Nearly three thousand years ago, Eskimos were skilled at carving walrus ivory, creating some of the most beautiful of all native American art. The carvings' small size and simplicity of line reflect the economy of the Eskimo lifestyle.

Early Russian explorers were struck by the hearty, robust appearance of the Eskimo. Davidof, a Russian officer who lived with the Eskimos in the late eighteenth century, describes a chief at Igak as standing six feet, nine inches tall. They had a strong sense of religion, and saw omens in natural events, all guided by spirits.

Belief in spirits also guided the lives of another of Alaska's native peoples, the Indians. Most numerous and widely scattered of these were the Athabascans. They were principally forest hunters and fishermen who, much like the Eskimos and the Aleuts, were masters of survival in their environment. The bow and arrow was used to hunt moose, caribou and bear, while traps and snares were used to capture smaller game. As a hedge against winter starvation, fish were taken from the rivers and dried. The Tanaina Indians of Cook Island, also part of the Athabascan nation, hunted sea mammals as well.

To the southeast lived the Tlingits and the Haidas. Like the Athabascans, the Tlingits hunted and fished. Unlike most of their northern neighbors, however, they had the twin benefits of plentiful resources and the warm Japan Current which flows north from California. This allowed the Indians of the southeastern Alaskan coast to develop as traders and craftsmen. Here the native culture of Alaska reached its pinnacle. The abundance of fish and game in warmer seasons made hunting easy and left time for creative expression through the use of cedar, spruce, leather, bone and other natural materials. Beautiful community homes ornamented with painted carvings adorned most villages. Men traveled the seas in graceful, red cedar canoes.

These people are probably best known for their totem poles, although the largest and most elaborate of these were not created until the nineteenth century, when white man's tools became available.

Totems came in many varieties: memorial poles, potlatch poles, mortuary poles, even farcical or ridicule poles. One of the most interesting totems is the famous Lincoln pole of Tongass village. It is the tribute of the Ganaxadi people to the great emancipator who, though dead by the time of the Alaska purchase, was credited by these "People of the Raven" with freeing them from slavery.

As in many early cultures, slavery was an accepted feature of community living among the Indians of the southern Alaskan coast and panhandle. It was not generally practiced by the Athabaskan tribes of the interior, however. Slaves are only of use in a settled society with established homes and plentiful food. The wandering northern tribes would have found themselves burdened with additional mouths to feed had they kept slaves.

At the time of the first European contact, Indian society was highly developed and complex. A strong caste system had taken hold, particularly among the Haidas and Tlingits of the south. All members of the tribe were People of the Wolf or Raven, depending on the group to which the mother belonged. Marriage was always between people of different groups. These groups were subdivided into lesser clans with different totems such as the Otter, Shark or Frog.

A person's social status depended on the potlatch, a party at which gifts were distributed to enhance the host's social standing. Potlatches might be held for any occasion such as a successful hunt, a wake or memorial, or the birth of a child.

Slaves were at the bottom of the social ladder. They were generally captured in the many wars fought by the quarrelsome Tlingits and later by the Haidas when the latter arrived in Alaska from the Queen Charlotte Islands of British Columbia in the early seventeenth century. Some of the lesser tribes and clans were largely made up of slaves or their descendants. By the early nineteenth century, one third of the Tlingits were slaves. Slavery did not end for the Indians until the American acquisition of the region in 1867, which brought the power of the thirteenth amendment to Alaska.

Indian borders tended to be relatively fluid in terms of European concepts of territory. Yes, territory was important, but survival and following game took first priority. The semi-nomadic Athabaskans occasionally fought wars over their hunting grounds but, like the Inuit, were not inclined to stay in one place.

The last Indian migration of any size occurred in 1887, when the Tsimshian Indians of British Columbia, under the leadership of tough Scots missionary William Duncan, reached an accord with the United States Government and resettled on Annette Island, a few miles south of Ketchikan. The Tsimshian Reservation on Annette Island was a remarkable success, with its sawmill, salmon cannery, homes, schools, and the largest church in Alaska.

Alaska's native peoples survived for thousands of years without contact with the outside world. Their lives are known to us through their art, which survives today in collections such as those at the University of Alaska in Fairbanks or at the Alaska State Museum in Juneau, where the original Lincoln totem can be seen. Alaska is keenly aware of its early heritage. Even small towns contain museums or collections of early Alaskan artifacts. From the several magnificent totem pole collections of Ketchikan, to the Visitor Information Center and Museum at Tok, Alaskans have done much to preserve their past.

The Northern Alaska Native Association has founded an incredible exhibit at Kotzebue in the Living Museum of the Arctic, with native Alaskans practising their traditional crafts and skills.

Much of this traditional Alaskan way of life was rudely jarred by the arrival of the first outsiders, the Russians.

In the eighteenth century, the Russians were hungry for status, via a place in the community of great nations. Hunger of any kind can be a powerful force for change. Being considered barely civilized by her neighbors, Russia could only expand one way in the quest for discovery and empire. To the west were the hostile Swedes and Poles. To the south was Russia's traditional enemy, Turkey. Only Siberia towards the east, and whatever lay beyond, was open to her.

It was the age of exploration.

By the end of the seventeenth century the Russians had established themselves in Siberia by adventure and conquest. Although the coveted fur trade belonged to them, the lucrative European market was too distant. Following the path of least resistance, the Russians usually traded furs in the Chinese markets to the south, in exchange for products such as tea and silks.

The subjugation of Siberia's natives and the corruption and inefficiency of the monopoly the state held on the Siberian fur trade did not promise the success that had accompanied the Spanish and Portuguese trade efforts in South America, the British and French efforts in eastern North America, or the Dutch efforts in the China Sea.

Now across the stage of Russian history strode a figure who

would change not only the face and destiny of Russia, but of the Arctic as well. Peter the Great, Russian Czar, shipwright, scientist, diplomat, world trader and consummately inquisitive man, was urged on by the foreign scientists and businessmen he had encouraged to reside in Russia to reach out for the American continent and see if it was joined to Siberia.

To command the first great Russian expedition to the New World Peter chose Vitus Bering, a Danish seaman in Russian service. For lieutenants, Bering had the services of Martin Spangberg, also a Dane, and Alexei Chirikov, a native Russian.

The object of the expedition, which was to build two ships on the Siberian coast, head north along that coast until some Europeans were contacted, and to draw up charts and sailing directions en route, may have sounded simple enough, but it proved to be a Herculean task. The expedition left St. Petersburg in three groups early in 1725. Heavy tools and iron for shipbuilding were to be carried by horses, men and river barges over 5,000 miles across unfamiliar territory. Frozen rivers, six-foot snows and near starvation almost ended the adventure for Spangberg's party.

Over three years passed before Bering's ship, the *Gabriel*, was launched. In 1728 he sailed north and found the strait separating Russia and Alaska that would later be named for him. Though he sailed to within a few miles of the Alaskan coast, Bering did not report seeing any major body of land other than St. Lawrence Island and the Siberian coast.

He was nonetheless convinced of the proximity of land to the east. The Chuckchee natives of Siberia talked of it. Driftwood collected on the beach provided still more evidence. With the political climate in Russia still conducive to science and exploration, Bering again proposed an expedition to the unknown lands to the east. Peter the Great had died in 1725 but his successors continued to encourage learning, and many foreign scientists still found favor at the royal court. Bering's wish was granted.

The second expedition would explore much new territory on both the Siberian and American coasts. Flora and fauna, as well as natural resources, were to be studied. Information about the inhabitants of new lands and their customs would be recorded. Spangberg, by now a veteran explorer, would cover the coast of Siberia south to Japan.

These were to be extremely complex explorations requiring years of preparation. Heavy responsibilities sat upon Bering's shoulders.

The Russians were not experienced in deep-sea voyaging, so instead of sailing from St. Petersburg around Europe and Africa into the Pacific, they chose to carry everything overland and down the Siberian rivers to the Pacific coast. There ships had again to be built on largely unfamiliar territory. To compound Bering's problems, squabbling often broke out between naval officers and officials. The scientists on the expedition occasionally displayed bursts of egotism which, combined with their foreign birth, often resulted in friction with the sensitive Russians.

At last, the summer of 1741 found Bering's expedition ready to go in search of northwestern America. His two ships – the *St. Paul*, under the command of Alexei Chirikov, and the *St. Peter*, commanded by Bering himself – were as well provisioned as conditions allowed. Unfortunately, both ships spent valuable time and supplies searching for "Gamaland," a mythical land assumed to be somewhere to the southeast.

When the commanders finally turned northeast, they became separated by storms. Chirikov and the *St. Paul* sailed almost due east until July 15, 1741, when the first sightings of land occurred at what is now called Prince of Wales Island, at the southern end of the Alaskan panhandle. There being no decent anchorage, the *St. Paul* continued north for two more days. Just when they thought a harbor and a landing place had at last been found, fate stepped in to provide one of Alaska's many unsolved mysteries.

Chirikov sent ten men under the command of his chief mate ashore in the longboat to see what lay ahead. The boat rounded a small spit of land and headed for what is probably today Sitka harbor.

Several days passed without a sign from the longboat's crew. Chirikov then sent the boatswain, carpenter, and five sailors in the ship's only other small boat to search for them. The following day, some Indians in canoes came out to examine the strange ship which had appeared in their waters, but paddled away before any contact was made.

The two small boats and eighteen men had vanished. The *St. Paul* searched for several days along the coast but no trace of them was ever found.

The *St. Paul* also had other problems – lack of fresh water and an outbreak of scurvy among the men. Curious Aleuts provided some fresh water as the *St. Paul* headed back along the Aleutian chain to Russia. Many men on board died from malnutrition and disease.

It was not until the spring of 1742 that Chirikov was able to take to sea again in search of the long overdue Bering.

Bering, in the *St. Peter*, had sailed somewhat north of the course taken by the *St. Paul*. He sighted land less than two days after Chirikov's discovery. Bering's first sight of Alaska was near present-day Yakutat on St. Elias's day, 1741, giving the name of that saint to the mountains he saw in the distance.

Bering landed a party on Kayak Island four days later. Acutely aware of winter's advance and the shortage of vegetables, Bering headed back towards Russia. In late August the first death from scurvy occurred aboard the *St. Peter*: Shumagin, a sailor, was buried on the island that bears his name. Again fate stepped in to give the story an ugly twist. Before Bering and his men could make home port they were shipwrecked.

Like the hapless Shumagin, Bering was to rest in a grave on an island that would bear his name. The survivors under Bering's second-in-command, Sven Waxel, a Swede, would eventually build a new ship from the wreckage of the *St. Peter* and sail home.

By 1742, the Bering expeditions were over. Bering and many of his men had died cold, hungry deaths. Also dead were Peter the Great and his successors Catherine I, Peter II and the Empress Anna. With them died the spirit of enlightenment that had made the explorations of the new world possible. Bering's lieutenants, mostly of foreign birth, found themselves out of favor in St. Petersburg. A great age had ended.

Only in later years did the work of these explorers become appreciated. The Russian expeditions to America were among the greatest ever mounted by a European power. They had cost vast hoards of treasure, and hundreds, perhaps thousands, of lives, yet they had opened the door to one of the richest and most challenging adventures in mankind's history, an adventure that in many ways continues today.

Alaska was to see a great deal more of the Russians, with or without the Imperial Government's sanction. Russian hunters and traders quickly became aware of the valuable furs that Bering's men had brought back. Soon cutthroats and thieves were competing with legitimate businessmen for the bounty of the Alaskan islands. The Russian Government was occupied with war in Europe and only turned a fleeting eye to the north Pacific when import duties or "tributes" (taxes) were due from the captive natives.

The Russian hand fell particularly heavily upon the Aleut people. As the furred animals disappeared from the outermost islands, the traders worked their way east to the mainland, treating the native population brutally.

The second half of the eighteenth century saw an increasing number of ships sail from the Russian base of Kamchatka for the American islands. Many of these ships had been quickly and poorly built. According to the Alaskan historian Clarence C. Hulley, an average of one out of three ships never returned.

The native people of the Aleutian Islands were now learning to deal with the traders. In 1762 the Aleuts ambushed a group of Russians who were ashore gathering skins. They nearly annihilated the shore parties on Umnak and Unalaska Islands and burned or sank four large ships. The traders, in turn, sought vengeance with a campaign of wholesale destruction.

The Russian invaders got an unfriendly reception on Kodiak Island as well. Here lived a warlike and independent Eskimo people that had evidently gotten the word about the strange white man in the big boats.

Empress Catherine II assumed the throne in 1762. Along with her European ways and manners she brought back some of the high regard for science that had been missing since the last government-sponsored expeditions to the Arctic regions. More explorations were undertaken and the Russians landed near present-day Nome around 1766. The Russian hold on this new conquest was tenuous and, in the early 'Seventies, Catherine II dropped the natives' obligatory "tribute" of furs, probably because it was now too costly to collect them.

By now, the Russians had competition for Alaska's resources. British Captain James Cook had landed on the Alaskan coast and had explored the islands. The British and the Yankees from New England had discovered north Pacific furs. Skilled mariners, they could not be kept from these seas, where the seal and sea otter abounded. Certainly the weak Russian presence was no obstacle to them.

In addition to belicose natives, hard weather, and Yankee sea rovers, the Russian traders had to deal with internal problems and pressures. The fierce rivalry between competing Russian companies was wasteful and inefficient, and occasionally led to bloodshed and piracy. Also, it was getting more difficult to fill the hold of a ship with prime skins. Earlier traders had been too greedy and had almost exhausted the Aleutians of this valuable commodity. The next move would have to be towards the mainland, with permanent settlements to maintain bases for collecting and trading furs. Grigory Shelekhov and his company built an outpost at Three Saints Bay on the northeast coast of Kodiak Island in 1784. This settlement became Alaska's first permanent European village.

In 1799, this company, was granted exclusive rights to the Russian fur trade in America. The Russian-American Company was a private monopoly with governmental blessing. It was to found settlements along the Pacific coast, maintaining Russia's territorial claims, and fending off foreign rivals such as the Hudson Bay Company to the east and the Spanish to the south.

Little is left from those early days of the Russian presence. Alaska is so big, it is perhaps harder to leave one's mark. What must be Alaska's oldest European structure, the Baranof House, originally a Russian commissary built in 1793, still stands in Kodiak by the ferry dock. It is a wonderful community museum today, with early native as well as Russian artifacts resting together in the old Russian building as if they have at last resolved their differences.

Sitka was founded in 1799 by the Russian-American Company. Here a fort was built, with storehouses and quarters. The local neighbors were the Tlingit Indians, who evidently took offense at the presence of this post. In 1802 they burned it down, killing over 400 of its defenders. Then, the Tlingits fell on a large hunting expedition returning from gathering otter pelts in the nearby islands. Over 200 Aleut hunters and Russians were killed. It required a full naval force to retake Sitka, or what remained of it, in 1804.

The Indians had done some trading with the "Boston men," as all American traders who now frequented the Alaskan coast were known in those days. Though hostile to the Russians, the Indians had learned to barter with these other white men and had acquired guns from them, the same guns that were used to take Sitka.

The Imperial Government and the Russian-American Company were powerless to keep the Yankees from poaching furs and trading in their territory. In 1821 the Czar banned commerce with foreigners along the Alaskan islands and coasts, but was soon forced to back down. Local officials were chartering American ships to carry their cargoes!

The first half of the nineteenth century saw more exploration of the coastline. Traders were having to go farther afield to find furs now. Soon these traders and explorers turned inland in this quest for commerce. In 1839 Alaska's Russian Governor, Ferdinand Von Wrangell, published the first map showing details of parts of the Alaskan interior including Mt. Tenada, known to us now as Mt. McKinley.

Temporary outposts were established, followed later by more permanent settlements in the Kuskokwin Basin. Much of the exploration of the interior would be accomplished by Alaskan-born men of mixed blood. Like the half-Indian trappers of New England and lower Canada in the eighteenth century, these individuals were often the best-equipped men to travel the back country. They were a colorful lot, with European names and manners, and a professed belief in Christianity. They could speak several languages, both foreign and native, and seemed perfectly at home sleeping under the stars beneath a bear skin.

These were the men who would teach the trappers, traders, explorers and later the gold diggers how to survive the rigors of the Alaskan winter. Many a tenderfoot would owe his life to this hardy breed. For dealing with often hostile Indians and Eskimos, for learning to subsist on the bounty of the forests and streams, and for avoiding the many dangers of the environment, these men were indispensable as guides and captained most of the pioneering expeditions into the interior.

Adding to the American presence were the whalers working the seas south of the Aleutians. By the 1840s American whaling ships had established themselves in the Bering Sea and beyond. In 1848 the whaler *Superior* passed through the Bering Straits to chase the bowhead whale. The Russians also attempted to build on the opportunity presented by these plentiful whales. Several Finnish ships in Russian service were sent to the Alaskan whaling grounds in the 1850s, but the effort was doomed by the outbreak of the Crimean War. Several of the Russian ships were sunk by the British, and the demands of war prevented their replacement.

The Civil War dealt a nearly fatal blow to the American whaling industry in Alaskan waters. A desperate Confederacy, unable to hold back advancing Northern armies, and poorly equipped to defeat the Union navy, turned to a new device in the war at sea. Contracting with British shipyards, Southern agents had built, or had converted from existing vessels, a series of warships. Originally conceived as ships to break the Union navy's blockade of Southern ports, these ships instead became commercial raiders.

One of these ships, the CS. S. *Shenandoah*, was ordered to Alaskan waters as the Civil War was about to end. The *Shenandoah* had been out of contact with the rest of the world for some time. Captain Waddell could not risk being seen on the American West Coast, and the Russian Government was in sympathy with the Union. In the summer of 1865 the Shenandoah destroyed thirty-eight unarmed American whaling ships. She had done nearly all her deadly work after the war was over.

Earlier, the threat of Confederate raiders in both the Atlantic and Pacific had forced many American shipowners to change their documentation to foreign flags. Several registered and flew the flag of the Kingdom of Hawaii, but to no avail. Insurance rates skyrocketed. The whaling industry never fully recovered, although commercial whaling continued in Alaskan waters until the last of the ships retired in the late 1960s.

War also rang the death knell of the Russian Empire in America. The Crimean War raged in Europe from 1854 to 1856. Russia was shown to be hopelessly obsolete militarily. Only a gentlemen's agreement between the Hudson Bay Company and the Russian-American Company, seconded by their respective governments, kept Alaska from invasion. The British, though they had the upper hand, were only too glad to accede to this agreement. They feared a Russian sale of Alaska to the Americans. The Russian and British companies had, by this time, learned to get along, but the American companies were numerous and less inclined to agreements or compromises. Also, the British knew the Russians to be incapable of any offensive actions against their territory in northwestern Canada, whereas the Americans were a new power and prone to rash actions. They had already fielded armies in Canada in 1775 and 1812 and seemed to be in an expansionist mood.

At the end of the Crimean War Russia was nearly bankrupt. Her society was in a shambles and people were demanding reform. The Russian-American Company was in no better condition and was about to fold. This would leave Alaska in the hands of the Imperial Government. The fur trade was in a dreadful condition due to overkill. Fish and ice were too perishable to be profitable alternatives and, like lumber, would have to be shipped great distances. The natives were still hostile, and the Europeans who lived there were resentful of the ill treatment they had received at the hands of the local officials.

To compound matters, gold was being whispered about in the interior. This was not a cause for joy back in St. Petersburg.

The discovery of gold would certainly mean a gold rush from the restless United States. This would cause friction with the Americans, and Russia would lose the only friend who could serve as a buffer with Britain. "The Russian and American peoples have no injuries to forget or remember," Czar Alexander II was quoted as saying in 1866.

The Czar was something of a student of history. He could plainly see the futility of trying to keep the world from changing. So many other empires had been made to look foolish by their rebellious former colonies. Alexander II was a practical man as Czars go. Given to bold action, he had freed the serfs in 1861. Now he would free Russia of its burden to the east, fatten the Imperial treasury, renew his friendship with the United States, and pull the tail of the British lion. He would sell Alaska.

There was little drama about the largest real estate deal in history. The Czar wanted to sell, and the Secretary of State for the United States wanted to buy. After some minor quibbling over price the figure of 7,200,000 dollars was agreed upon.

Authorization from St. Petersburg arrived the evening of March 29, 1867 in Washington, D. C. The Russian Ambassador, Edouard de Stoeckl, and Secretary of State William Seward, wrestled with the language of the treaty until about 4 a. m. the next day: Congress was about to adjourn and would be impatient to go home. It was the best of times to gain their consent.

The Russian flag was lowered for the last time at Sitka on October 18, 1867. A contingent of American troops watched the local Russians "going about the town in a most dejected manner," carrying their possessions down to the docks to return to Russia. They left behind a century of memories. They also left behind the Russian Orthodox faith and a few of its beautiful churches.

St. Michael's Cathedral, in the heart of Sitka on Lincoln Street, burned down in 1966 but has been rebuilt exactly like the 1844 original. As it burned, citizens rushed into the building to rescue the famous Sitka Madonna icon and some of the most beautiful religious art in North America. Still an active church, St. Michael's welcomes visitors. Other handsome Russian churches can be seen in Kenai and Kodiak as well as St. Paul in the Pribilof Islands in the Bering Sea.

The American public's reaction to the Alaska purchase was generally favorable. It was hard to argue against acquiring property of any sort at two cents an acre. There were some who wanted to call the territory "Walrussia" or "Icebery." Skeptics also coined the term "Seward's Folly." But the new land to the north would soon be all but forgotten by the majority of the American people. Unfortunately, even the government seemed to be unconcerned with Alaska for much of the rest of the nineteenth century.

Americans often display a sort of missionary zeal about bringing civilization and progress to a new place. However, this feeling does not always last much beyond an initial burst of energy. So it was with Alaska after the purchase.

To replace the decayed Russian autocracy, the United States Government sent the United States Army. The small Alaskan population numbered perhaps 30,000 souls at the time, including approximately 24,000 natives. These residents, whether Russian, American, of mixed blood, or native, were considered a wild and independent lot, not inclined towards civilized society or politics. Aside from an early attempt to regulate imports and customs duties by the Treasury Department, few laws were passed.

Sitka made a half-hearted attempt at establishing civil law by electing a city council and a mayor in late 1867. Sitka became something of a boom town with drifters, gamblers, small-time merchants and adventurers of both sexes shipping in from San Francisco, Seattle and points south. But there wasn't much interest in municipal government among these newcomers, and the old-timers thought they could get along just fine without laws, schools and taxes. Issues of fairness, justice or vengeance had generally been settled man-to-man. Frontier law was not found in law books.

The army was not given very complete instructions on how to run things either. They had been given the task of maintaining order without the laws or judicial power necessary for that task. The courts of Oregon refused jurisdiction as well.

The job of patrolling the coast fell to the Revenue Cutter Service, later to be known as the Coast Guard. One of the things generally agreed on was the need to halt the smuggling of liquor into Alaska. Drunkenness and its attendant vices were a dominant problem in the settlements. Whiskey was used to "grease the wheels" of nearly every trade or transaction with the natives, whose tolerance for alcohol was somewhat lower than that of the hard-drinking white traders. Misunderstandings occurred frequently and often ended in violence. Prohibition was put into effect, though with virtually no success.

Drug smuggling, often thought of as a modern problem, was also to cause trouble. One enterprising fellow in this trade was James Carroll, a popular schooner captain who sailed up from British Columbia with whiskey and opium. When he was finally apprehended, his warehouse at Kasaan on Prince of Wales Island was opened. The authorities found illegal whiskey and trade goods along with 3000 pounds of opium. He was fined for his bad behavior.

Several years later, in 1889, Carroll appeared before a congressional committee in Washington, D. C. where he urged the Revenue Cutter Service to save its money and not bother with new, faster ships. Smuggling, he told them, was done in small, slow canoes.

Army administration was not much of a success in Alaska. The coastal nature of nearly all the settlements and towns called for ships, not soldiers. What's more, soldiers who had been shut up in cold army outposts with little to do often behaved in ways not befitting their stations. They were frequently more troublesome than the citizens.

Christmas of 1869 in Wrangell saw a drunken fight between

soldiers and Indians turn into a brief bombardment of the native village. Within a few months all Army posts were closed except for the one at Sitka. Army rule ended officially in 1877.

The Army was gone. Washington fumbled around for a way to bring democracy to Alaska. With the departure of the Army, the territory was left with only one land-based government offical, civil or military, the customs inspector at Sitka. The U. S. Navy stepped in until the Treasury Department could get a grip of the problem. The Treasury Department then gave the job of maintaining order to the Revenue Cutter Service. As in the case of the Army, the Revenue Cutter Service simply did not have the tools to do the job.

In the midst of the administrative void, Alaska came close to an Indian war. In 1879 a serious outbreak of violence occurred in Sitka. The Tlingits were angered, and justifiably so, by the deaths of several of their fellows when the American schooner they were working on sank in the Bering Sea in 1877. The ship's owners had refused to pay compensation to the families of the victims.

Throughout the winter of 1878 and 1879 friction grew between the white settlers and the natives. The whites finally sent a petition to the authorities in Victoria, British Columbia, asking for immediate aid. With permission from Washington, D. C., the British Government despatched the H.M.S. *Osprey* north to Sitka. Shortly thereafter it was relieved by the U.S.S. *Jamestown*. Order, of a fashion, was restored to the settlement.

There was no better way of getting the attention of the American public than to have a British ship rescue Americans on American soil. The American public was duly ashamed of their neglect. Or at least they were for a short time.

Attempts were made to bring order out of chaos by Captain Beardslee of the *Jamestown* with the help of Alaskans of all colors. Another attempt at self-government was made in Sitka in 1879. Like the first, it failed, but men of conscience were now living in Alaska and would be ready to take responsibility when the time came.

Missionaries at Wrangell had organized a police force from the Indian population. The prospects seemed encouraging until "demon rum" again intervened.

Visiting Indians from Admiralty Island had arrived with a plentiful supply of home-made whiskey. Soldiers had taught them to distill spirits. These were the Hoochenoo Indians and they would give the world the slang name for liquor, hootch.

The Indian police arrived to confiscate the illegal spirits and a riot started. The Hoochenoos couldn't have cared less about the missionaries' laws. An old-time shoot-out, complete with six-guns, ensued, but with few casualties. The combatants were in no condition to aim. By giving presents to the rival chiefs, Captain Beardslee managed to smooth things over.

Citizen police forces were generally not effective. They lacked a legal system and courts to back their peace-keeping efforts. In the case of smuggling and prohibition, very few Alaskans had any desire to stop the one or enforce the other. At least one early police force, formed to enforce the liquor laws, celebrated their installation of a police chief by having a drunken debauch for several days.

At least one chapter in this tough era ended only recently. In 1882, a native from Angoon on Admiralty Island, working aboard an American whaling ship, was killed while handling a "bomb lance" used to kill whales. Members of his tribe, knowing the dismal record white men's companies had for compensating bereaved families, grabbed two hostages and demanded 200 blankets for their loss.

The Navy sent a landing party to Angoon, along with the Revenue Cutter *Corwin*, and demanded 400 blankets from the natives for their offense. They refused. After determining the village of Angoon to have been evacuated by the Indians, the *Corwin* fired upon it. Then, Navy personnel went ashore and burned much of the village. The Indians sued the United States Government, but it wasn't until 1974 that they were awarded the sum of 90,000 dollars.

Laws were few in Alaska in the 1870s and 1880s. Means of enforcing those laws were even fewer. Only the Alaskan panhandle received any attention from the Navy or customs agents. The Pribilof Islands in the Bering Sea came under a special classification and were occasionally visited by a Revenue Cutter bringing supplies to the resident agent. What might be happening at Kotzebue or Barrow, Eskimo villages on the northwest coasts, only God and the Eskimos knew, and they weren't telling. The legacy of those days is a continuing rivalry between the southern coast of Alaska and the northern and interior regions of the state.

There was, however, change in the air for Alaska. The popular imagination of the American public was beginning to turn northward. James Gordon Bennett of *The New York Herald* sponsored an expedition to reach the North Pole.

In 1879, the expedition commander, a young naval officer named George Washington De Long hired two Indians from St. Michael, Alaska, as hunters and dog drivers, and headed through the Bering Strait aboard the *Jeanette*, a tired, wooden sailing ship with an auxiliary steam engine. The crew was ill-prepared for the events of the next two years.

In September of 1879 the ship froze in the ice east of Wrangell Island. They had, in the meantime, discovered and named nearby Herald Island. Briefly freed from the ice, they were soon stuck again, and were no closer to their goal.

The pack ice that held them was now crushing the *Jeanette*, so the men got out onto the ice with their sleds, boats and supplies. Somewhere in the wreckage of the ship the casks of lime juice, so essential to the prevention of scurvy, were lost.

On June 17, 1881, the *Jeanette* sank. The next morning the party began their trek over the ice, heading south. Bearing heavy loads over treacherous ice they traveled slowly, covering five and a half miles in eight days. The men were never told, but De Long, in taking bearings, found the drifting ice had actually carried them 25 miles further north!

Eventually they began sighting islands and landed on one of them, Kotelni Island, far north of Siberia. Here they took to their boats, which they had been carrying by sled.

Only one of the boats made it to safety. De Long himself did not. Three years after his death some of his supplies were found on the ice by an Eskimo. The supplies had traveled thousands of miles on the ice floe, finally to be picked up in West Greenland.

Inland Alaska had barely been visited by non-natives up to this time. The Athabaskan Indians had maintained almost sole proprietorship of this rich land. Only the occasional prospector or explorer would pass through.

The aggressive Scots traders of the Hudson Bay Company had established posts at Fort Yukon and Fort Selkirk in the 1840s, but they had pulled out, heading for Canada in 1869, and leaving only a small store in the hands of an American. In 1883 the United States Army sent Lieutenant Fredrick Schwatka to explore the Alaskan interior. Subsequent expeditions even began to use river steamers.

Explorers and traders were not the only people concerned with the North. Missionaries had been part of Alaskan life for many years.

The Reverend Sheldon Jackson was not the first Protestant missionary to come to Alaska, but he was one of the most influential. He was soon bringing more missionaries to Alaska and planning schools. When the United States Government finally took things in hand and passed the Alaska Government Act of 1884, Jackson was awarded the post of Special Agent for the Bureau of Education.

A clumsy man with strong opinions, he was arrested in Sitka for his high-handed manner in organizing a school, but he nevertheless proved to be an effective pioneer for education. Soon schools had been established at Barrow in the far north and at Point Hope in the northwest.

The Moravians founded a mission at Bethel in the Kuskokwin valley in 1885 and their influence is still felt as present-day Bethel is "dry."

Roman Catholic missions appeared in the middle Yukon basin as early as 1886. Bishop Sehger, the man responsible for the first Catholic missionary expedition into the interior, was killed by a crazed miner before completing his work. Two years later Father Robaut founded the mission school at Holy Cross, on the Yukon River. Here in 1899 he printed the first school primer in the Eskimo language.

The Episcopalians founded a mission near Anvik in 1886, and were instrumental in organizing hospitals at Nenana, Fort Yukon and Wrangell. The Reverend J. L. Prevost founded the Episcopal mission at Tanana and printed the *Yukon Press* in January, 1894, the first paper published north of Juneau.

Methodists opened an orphanage at Unalaska, later moving to Seward. Quakers founded schools at Kotzebue and other northern villages. The forces of civilization were finally on the march to Alaska.

Alaska has always had the allure of the pot of gold at the end of a rainbow. Periodically, Alaska has had its waves of get-rich-quick schemers who show up with empty pockets and hopeful smiles. First the furs enticed them, then the whales. Canneries were opening on the coast, where cheap labor and fish abounded.

Few tax benefits accrued to Alaska from all this. In the eyes of some, Alaska might as well have been a colony of Seattle. The territory's second governor, Alfred P. Swineford, was quoted as saying in 1885 that Alaska was "a national fat goose left unprotected and annually plucked of its valuable plumage by non-resident corporations."

Natives on the Aleutians and to the north were now beginning to suffer shortages due to the imprudent way in which the seal, walrus, whale and even caribou had been hunted by the white man.

But Alaska was becoming more aware of itself. Progressive men were beginning to take control. Pelagic sealing was being brought under control. Siberian reindeer were imported to help provide subsistence for hungry Eskimos on the Seward Peninsula. Courts and town councils had been established. Then the word got out about the gold.

Gold was not unknown in Alaska before the 1890s. But the territory's interior had been largely inaccessible until the late nineteenth century. The region's mineral wealth was never open to question. Coal had been picked up on the north coast near Cape Lisburne. Copper had been found by Army explorers in the Chitina Valley. The Russians had hard evidence of gold in the early nineteenth century, and enterprising American prospectors were braving the Chilkat Indian domination of Chilkoot Pass in the 1870s to see what the streams of the Yukon might yield.

The first strike was in the summer of 1880. Dick Harris and Joe Juneau found gold-bearing quartz along the banks of the Gastineau Channel. The spot developed into a boom town overnight. The richest areas around the new town of Juneau were quickly claimed, so the novice miners headed inland. Six years later, another rich strike occurred, this time just over the border in the Yukon.

The boom in Juneau petered out but the town did not wither. In 1906 the territorial capital was moved from Sitka to Juneau.

Circle City was probably the first boom town of the Alaskan Yukon area. In 1893 a prospector from New Hampshire and two natives found gold near Birch Creek. Within two years Circle City was the largest mining town in the interior. Today it is quiet, boasting a trading post with camping and fishing supplies, hunting gear and licenses. There is a helicopter pad for tours, and a good saloon. What more could you ask for?

During the gold rush era, the most popular route into the Canadian Yukon was through Skagway. In the summer of 1898 this town was probably the largest in Alaska. While Canada, just up the road over White Pass, was handling the gold rush with order and dignity thanks to the Mounties, Skagway was behaving in time-honored Alaskan tradition. That is, it was not behaving at all.

Skagway had fallen under the spell of a redoubtable character named Jefferson R. "Soapy" Smith. This worthy had appeared in Skagway fresh from a boatload of novice miners in the fall of 1897 looking for opportunity. He had a way of ingratiating himself with people who could be of some service to him.

On the way to Alaska aboard the steamer *City of Seattle*, a young man accidentally cast loose a navigation light hanging in the rigging. The light crashed down square on the head of a hapless greenhorn, putting *his* light out for good. The future miners, who were most of the passengers, became very upset and called a miners' meeting to discuss a lawsuit against the steamship company and captain.

In stepped Smith. He looked at the body stretched out on a table in front of the assembled crowd. First he asked if anyone knew the departed. No one did. Then he announced that the fellow was a stowaway and had stolen Smith's medal and a package from him.

As he made this declaration he produced a medal and a small package from the unfortunate's pocket with his own "J. R. Smith" on them. He then said he had no use for a crowd who would stand up for a thief and walked away. The crowd drifted away, quite deflated. The ship's master, Captain Hunter, thought Smith a capital fellow.

Smith soon had a gang of toughs in Skagway running crooked shell games, fleecing gullible newcomers, committing robberies and probably worse. He was careful, however, not to make the wrong enemies. He put together a body of men he referred to as the "First Regiment, Alaska Militia," and offered them, with himself as Colonel of course, to President McKinley for the Spanish American War. The President declined the offer.

A number of murders ended Soapy's days in Skagway. It was suspected that his gang was responsible for these crimes and a meeting of concerned citizens was called. Soapy was furious. He grabbed his rifle and headed over to the meeting. He had been drinking and he picked a fight with Frank Reid, the man who was guarding the door outside the meeting.

Soapy Smith died with a bullet in his heart. Twenty-six of his cohorts were rounded up later. Frank Reid also died from bullet wounds. Both men are still in Skagway. They rest near one another in Gold Rush Cemetery. Frank Reid's tombstone is inscribed: "He died for the honor of Skagway. "

The population of Alaska doubled between 1890 and 1900. River boats were working up and down the Yukon River from St. Michael on the coast to the junction of the Charley River and almost to the Canadian border. In 1896 a major gold strike happened in the Klondike over in Canada.

The early "sourdoughs," as the miners were called, had a backbreaking job ahead of them. Panning for gold in streams, or washing the sand away from the heavier gold that settles in a miner's pan, was long work with a small return.

Mining for gold could mean huge profits, but the digging was done by hand. After digging down through the topsoil, miners encountered permafrost. This had to be melted with fires or hot rocks. The dirt was removed by hand-hauled buckets and was then washed in sluice boxes to separate the gold. It was hit or miss. Beginning in 1898, steam was used for thawing the ground.

1898 was a big year in Alaska's history. The Klondike and Alaskan gold strikes were now big news around the world.

Thousands of would-be mineral millionaires flocked to the northwest. The United States Government, worried about starvation, approved a two million dollar expenditure for emergency food supplies. It was not necessary.

This was also the year of the birth of Nome, the result of another rich strike. Known as the Cape Nome Mining District, or Anvil, within a few weeks of the discovery of gold it had become a shantytown built of Civil War surplus tents, old sails or tarpaulin, and driftwood.

In the midst of a series of disputes about the legality of some of the Nome claims, gold was found on the beach. It was the easiest money imaginable. Gold could literally be shovelled out of the sand.

Nome had gone from a population of a few Eskimos and a trader in 1897 to a huge gypsy camp of 12,488 people in June of 1900. Several thousand more were in the vicinity rooting in the sand and probing the streams for the magic yellow metal. People slept anywhere. A haphazard form of city government sprang up. People were threatened with arrest if they did not use the public latrines that had recently been dug. Tickets to these conveniences could be purchased for ten cents each or three for a quarter. This colorful era is well represented at the Carrie McClain Museum on Front Street in modern Nome.

Smaller gold strikes continued into the present century, though without the romance of the past. Fairbanks began as a gold strike by two Italian miners in 1901. Like Circle to the northeast, Fairbanks became a boom town, although by now Alaskans were learning to handle the situation with more grace.

Nevertheless, the usual collection of con men, peddlers and gamblers were on hand; Fairbanks even had its own highwayman known as the "Blue Parka Bandit" who skulked about in the bushes on the roads leading to town. He once stopped Bishop Rowe but, upon realizing who the esteemed clergyman was, he returned his money and gave a little extra for the church. He was a member of the Bishop's parish.

Fire destroyed Fairbanks in 1906. By 1909, however, the town could count 3,000 souls plus another 8,000 or 9,000 in the immediate vicinity. They had a full complement of churches, schools and businesses, a theater, three newspapers and a choral society. The cultural life of Fairbanks was remarkable for its day and it is still a state leader in the performing arts. The city is home to the University of Alaska, the Alaska Music Festival, the Fairbanks Symphony and the Light Opera Theater.

Alaska was maturing as the new century dawned. Economically, Alaska had more diversity than in the past. Whaling was by now almost nonexistent, and the fur trade was no longer lucrative, but salmon fishing and its attendant canneries were doing well. Alaska's canneries developed in the late 1870s and were in full operation when gold began to lose its luster.

The famous Alaska Packers fleet of sailing ships graced the Pacific coast until the age of the sailing ships passed. Like the sea otter which had been hunted to extinction, the salmon was being caught with little regard for the future. Absentee ownership of the industry resulted in resentment between Alaskan fishermen and the packers. "Fish pirates" robbed the traps of the canneries and occasionally shot it out with the Packers' guards. The United States Navy was sent north with patrol boats at the end of World War I to keep order. Conservation did not become an issue in the business until the 1920s. It still sparks controversy.

Gold was not the only mineral to enrich Alaska's past. Beginning in 1908, Alaska had a copper industry along the Copper River and in the Wrangell mountains. The Alaska Syndicate which owned the copper mines also built the Alaska Steamship Company with a fleet of 17 modern ships.

The city of Anchorage, now Alaska's largest, began life as a construction camp in 1913. This was not another gold rush boom town. Anchorage was a planned town, a base for the construction of the Alaska Railroad. It has grown particularly fast since World War II and the subsequent oil boom of the 1960s.

On March 27, 1964 an earthquake, lasting for over three minutes, struck the Alaskan coast. Anchorage, along with Valdez and Kodiak, was nearly destroyed. The shock was followed by a tidal wave that swept the town of Valdez away. Traces of this destruction remain, but Anchorage did not mourn its plight for long. Rebuilding began immediately, and Alaska's "Big Apple" continued to grow and prosper.

Home to Alaska Pacific University, as well as a branch of the University of Alaska, Anchorage is becoming a center for Pacific studies, drawing students and teachers from Asia, Samoa and Hawaii. A clean, modern city, Anchorage is a surprise to many newcomers to Alaska.

Alaska's greatest period of growth in the modern era occurred during World War II. New road systems were built and more of Alaska became accessible. Airfields were established in Nome and Fairbanks for the delivery of planes to Russia. A naval base was set up at Dutch Harbor. Mining came to a halt, and young Alaskans went off to war.

Despite these rather tardy preparations for war, Alaska was vulnerable to attack. The attack came at dawn, June 3, 1942. What followed became one of the strangest military campaigns in which the United States ever became involved.

Carrier-based planes of the Imperial Japanese Navy attacked first at Dutch Harbor on Unalaska Island. Two days of attacks caused great damage, but Army Air Corps planes from the base at Umnak responded and the Japanese flew back to their carriers under cover of fog.

The Japanese Navy now turned west in the thick fog. They next struck at Attu and Kiska at the end of the Aleutian chain. The few islanders were captured and sent to Japan as prisoners. The Japanese dug in for a long siege.

American bombers pounded the islands through the winter of 1942 and into 1943. The navy shelled the islands as well. On May 11, the Americans "hit the beach" at Attu. After a month of fighting from rock to rock, the island was retaken. The entire Japanese garrison had been wiped out.

Kiska was next. For weeks it was bombarded by air and by sea. Finally, American and Canadian troops stormed ashore. It was the 15th of August. They found the island deserted. Only two friendly dogs were there to greet the liberators. Under cover of the dense Aleutian fog, the Japanese fleet had evacuated its troops and slipped silently away a month earlier.

After the war, Alaska emerged as a very different place from what it had been before. New pioneers were settling Alaska now, men and women who had first experienced Alaska during the war. These were not the get-rich-quick schemers of gold rush days. The Alaska of Soapy Smith and his ilk was receding into the past. "The Great Land" had found a solid place for itself in the life of the republic. Now, Alaskans wanted recognition. The long climb for political equality had begun in 1884 with limited self-government. In 1906, at the behest of President Theodore Roosevelt, Alaska was granted a nonvoting representative in Congress.

Lobbying for statehood began in 1916. Alaska became the 49th State in the Union in 1959.

Alaska is by far the largest state in the Union, with 375 million acres – an area as large as all the Western states combined. Despite its vast size, its entire population is that of a medium-sized city, with well over half its citizens living in urban areas.

Within Alaska's huge expanse of territory are glaciers and fjords, and about 3,000,000 lakes including Iliamna, the second largest freshwater lake in America. Alaska also claims the highest peak in North America, Mount McKinley, rising 20,320 feet above Denali National Park.

Set apart from the lower forty-eight states, awesome in size and sheer physical beauty, Alaska has had to face some monumental problems unique to the far north.

The conservation of resources has never been a strong priority with the companies who have made their money in the territory. Uphill battles have been waged to keep companies from overhunting, overfishing or overcutting Alaskan resources. Salmon spawning grounds have had to be protected, certain types of traps banned, and the clear cutting of timber halted, all in the face of formidable opposition from industry lobbies. The battle continues today.

Another ongoing dispute concerns land use. Environmentalists warn of the possible dangers from development to the balance of nature in Alaska. They say the rugged country to the far north is deceptively delicate, that the vast areas of wilderness are necessary and desirable assets for all Americans. Development-minded Alaskans, also concerned about Alaska's future, claim these fears are exaggerated.

Caught up in the growth process of the 49th State are its aboriginal, or native, citizens. Often pushed aside or exploited, they were rarely considered when there was a dollar to be made. For many years Alaska even maintained separate school systems for them. Then, in 1945, the state legislature passed an anti-discrimination bill. No longer could someone be refused the use of public accommodations because of race or color. Today, Alaska's population of approximately 410,000 includes some 60,000 natives.

The discovery of oil and the construction of the Alaska pipeline moved the natives to push for justice. The issue of land use and ownership was, at last, met head-on. In 1971 the Alaska Native Claims Settlement Act awarded the original Alaskans forty-four million acres of land and 962. 5 million dollars. The money and property continues to be administered by thirteen regional corporations set up by the natives.

Another problem facing them is how to maintain the skills and traditions of the past in the face of progress, with its modern conveniences and educational opportunities. The conflict and its resulting frustrations have sparked an increase in alcoholism and crime. But the natives of Alaska are not waiting for solutions to be imposed upon them. Over fifty native villages have passed laws against the sale of alcohol. They have shown that skilled craftsmen and hunters can also be businessmen and legislators.

Oil is not a new commodity to Alaska. Surface deposits had been noticed by the first pioneers to the area in the nineteenth century. Wildcatters actually drilled wells early in the twentieth century, and a small refinery was built near Cordova. Oil was found in several locations in Alaska but the biggest discovery came with the Prudhoe Bay strike in 1968. The state immediately cashed in by selling millions of dollars in oil leases.

Environmentalists warned against the abuse of the land, citing the industrial history of the lower forty-eight states as an example. Most Alaskans seemed to feel that they could have the blessings of industry and still retain their closeness to nature. The stage was set for confrontation and the argument still continues. In the meantime, the pipeline from Prudhoe Bay is sending oil south to the tanker port at Valdez.

Alaska is not just America's last frontier. It is our past and our future. The pride, the shame, the sorrow and the joy of Alaska's history is our own. It has been a land of pioneers and prophets. Now universities stand on the sites of mining camps, and the Alaska Repertory Theater tours where once even trappers could not go.

The Aleuts of long ago called this place "The Great Land" from which we have the name Alaska. Stand anywhere near the mountain the Indians called *Denali* – Mount McKinley – and look toward its snow-covered peak.

They were right.

Previous page: a sky so blue it seems within reach is reflected in a lake swollen by snowmelt beside the Richardson Highway between Delta Junction and Valdez. Sizeable, but not ostentatious, the Governor's mansion (right) stands on an ordinary street in the state capital, Juneau. Juneau was founded after the prospectors Richard Harris and Joe Juneau struck a fabulously rich gold seam in the area in 1880 – streaks of solid gold running through the rock were incredulously recorded by one of the men. Despite their initial good fortune, however, neither man reaped his just reward; in fact, Juneau died so poor that a public collection was required to send his body back to the city he co-founded.

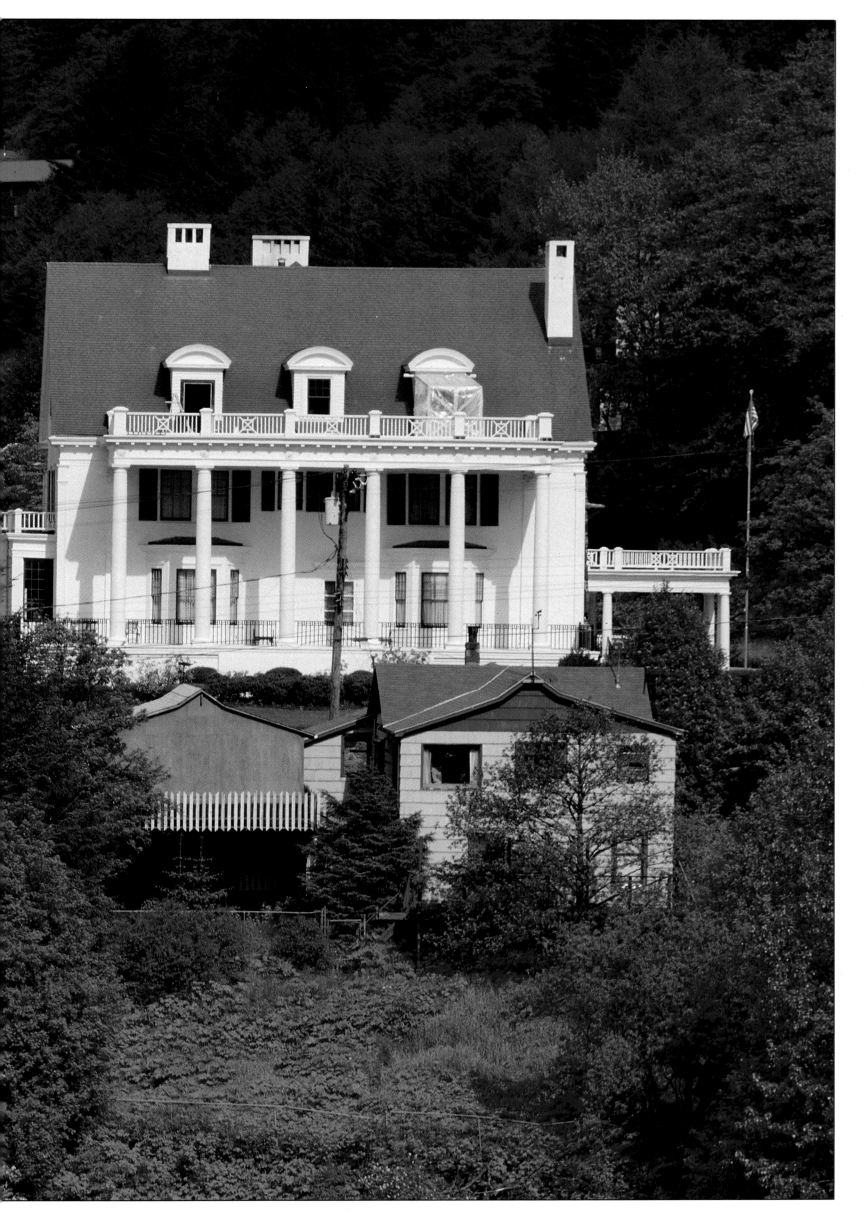

A quaint, evocative replica of an early log cabin church set beside office blocks of concrete and glass, the Juneau Visitor Center (facing page top) was built in 1980 for the city's centennial celebrations. Timber is a major resource in the Alaskan Panhandle and, in general, wooden buildings suit this rugged terrain; many of the city's houses (facing page bottom and above) are timber clad, appearing in harmony with surrounding mountain forests.

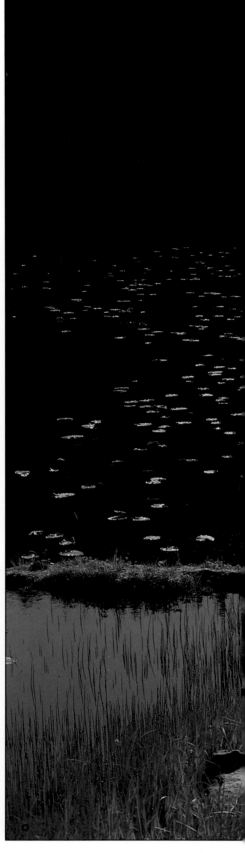

Living in a city accessible only by air or water, the inhabitants of Juneau (left) are accustomed to using float planes (above) or pleasure craft (overleaf) as their automobiles. Since the state can boast three million lakes, it has no shortage of "parking lots." Above left: fresh air and a fine view for a skier at the Eaglescrest Ski Area, twelve miles from Juneau on Douglas Island. Operating all year round, the resort offers a spectacular 1,400-foot ski drop and 640 acres of alpine skiing. Overleaf: almost perfect reflections in Auke Bay, which lends its name to a small town just outside Juneau at the head of the Lynn Canal.

Confronted by its massive size, it is comforting
to remember that the Mendenhall Glacier (right
and overleaf) is melting faster than it can
advance. Just fifty years ago this glacier covered
the land upon which much of Juneau now stands;
since then this ice river has retreated, today
ending thirteen miles from the city center. Fed by
the extensive Juneau Icefield, which lies to the
north of the capital, this is one of the most
famous glaciers in the world, partly because it is
so accessible. The visitor has the choice of floating
past it in an inflatable raft, landing on it by
helicopter, "flight-seeing" over it by bush plane
or just sitting in a car in the parking lot while
trying to comprehend the enormity of it. Then,
the rumors that the weather will turn colder to
bring the glacier down the path towards Juneau
again are best forgotten.

Above: at first glance similar to the smooth slabs of rock on which they sprawl, female northern fur seals bask in the summer sun in Glacier Bay National Park, while dominant males remain upright and alert, challenging all comers within their individual territories. Fur seals are common in the waters off the Alaskan coast, returning annually to the same breeding sites, some of which can be found in Glacier Bay National Park (above left), where (left), dwarfed by a massive boulder, a black bear pauses on a shoreline strewn with glacial moraine. Only occasionally is the beautiful subspecies of the black bear known as the "Glacier Blue" sighted amid the trees as it is both shy and rare.

Trees soften a mountainside clawed by a retreating glacier in Glacier Bay National Park. This bay, on the southeast coast of Alaska, began to form just two hundred years ago. Before then, there wasn't a bay here at all, just a solid wall of impenetrable ice. In the face of a series of earthquakes and a general warming of the area's climate, the wall began to melt and retreat – indeed, nowhere else in Alaska have tidewater glaciers receded as fast. Despite the comparatively recent departure of the ice, many of the slopes of Glacier Bay are already reclaimed by rain forest, home for some of the park's two hundred species of birds.

Above left and left: Adams Inlet and (above) Muir Inlet, both in Glacier Bay National Park, a truly wondrous place. Initial impressions suggest that nothing could move these huge monoliths of ice, yet in the silence it is possible to hear them creaking and sighing, whispered evidence of their progress. Suddenly, an enormous part of the serrated wall may break away and fall, with a sound like a thunderclap, into the bay. During the summer the wash from such a splash will rock boats half a mile away. In winter, those who choose to approach the glacier's snout across the bay's thick ice can find that the ice is broken up by the underwater shock waves after the glacier "calves," leaving such foolhardy explorers adrift.

Battened down against the winter gales, pleasure boats in Valdez harbor are prepared for rough weather, though a fishing vessel remains ready to sail with the tide. In December and January, winter daylight arrives mid morning and has faded to dusk by mid afternoon, so much of the daily routine has to be undertaken in darkness. Boats are far more common than cars, and of far more use, since comparatively little of Alaska is under tarmac, but many towns are accessible by sea or river. Valdez itself was rebuilt after a mighty earthquake razed the city in 1964, and today it is perhaps best known as the destination of the Trans-Alaska Pipeline. Overleaf: a sunset of tropical intensity over Mineral Creek, a waterway that flows from a glacier of the same name north of Valdez.

As every Alaskan knows, the Trans-Alaska Pipeline stretches 800 miles from Prudhoe Bay, within the Arctic Circle, to Valdez on the Gulf of Alaska. Completed by 1977, the construction of the pipe took just two years. Some sections of it were carried above ground (above) to avoid its heat melting the permafrost, as tundra soils will erode if thawed. The line's characteristic zig-zag path (overleaf) contributes to its flexibility in the face of heat expansion or earthquakes, and information boards (above left and left) stud the route to explain the pipe's purpose and construction to the public.

A river gorge in the Chugach Mountains near Valdez. This land looks empty, but it is actually teeming with wildlife – a quiet pause of just half an hour or so is sure to reveal some of the creatures that inhabit the Alaskan interior. The river will be rich in salmon in their season, the forest is the haunt of grizzly bears, arctic foxes, lynx and wolves, while the lakes, such as those (overleaf) along the Richardson Highway, shelter beaver, and in summer are frequented by browsing moose. In sharp blue skies golden eagles soar all year, scouring the lower slopes of the mountains for snowshoe hares, unwary arctic ground squirrels or willow ptarmigan. Certainly, this is not the barren wasteland it at first appears; if nothing else, in that half an hour the insect population will have made itself felt!

From the Richardson Highway (above), the peaks of the Alaskan Range, marbled in snow above the tree line, look forbidding even in high summer. The range, which stretches in an arc of some 650 miles from Iliamna Lake to the White River, contains Mount McKinley, the highest mountain on the North American continent. At the foot of these mountains, just over 150 miles from the Arctic Circle, in the Delta River region (above left and left), the Alaskans are farming the land. Cereals, such as barley and oats, ripen during the brief growing season by making the best use of the state's daily twenty-four hours of summer light. Locally, the barley harvest serves as important winter fodder for cattle, while generally, during the ten years of this project's development, the Delta area has played a significant part in Alaska's agricultural progress.

Above: the majestic peak of Mount Kimball rises to over 10,000 feet amid summits of the Alaskan Range iced as blue as the sky. Not far from here, at Isabel Pass on the Richardson Highway, the snow may thaw to reveal a bronze plaque set in stone (above right) that commemorates General Wilds P. Richardson, the first president of the Alaskan Road Commission. This organization was responsible for updating the Valdez-to-Fairbanks trail to automobile standards in the 1920s, hence the highway's name. Right: the 12,000 feet of Mount Drum challenge the little planes of Gulkana, a small town on the Richardson Highway. Bridging the state's vast distances is one of the greatest problems in Alaska – although all towns and cities are accessible by air, due to the miles between them, each is still obliged to be a self-contained unit.

The soft light of the morning sun warms low-roofed Fairbanks homes swaddled by the Chena River. Fairbanks was founded as a supply post for goldminers in the early 1900s and now forms the state's "Golden Heart" as a center of trade and finance. This seemingly isolated interior city also boasts the nation's northernmost university, the University of Alaska Fairbanks, founded in 1917, plus a number of military bases. The latter were established during the Second World War, when U.S. soldiers built a road to connect apparently vulnerable Alaska with the "Lower 48" of the contiguous United States. The road, the great Alaskan Highway, ended at Fairbanks – and the city never looked back. Indeed, construction has continued to favor Fairbanks: the laying of the Trans-Alaska Pipeline close to the city brought considerable prosperity in the 1970s.

Facing page top: a stern-wheeler on the Tanana River, southeast of Fairbanks – the entrepreneur E.T. Bartlett disembarked from a similar vessel to found the city in 1903. Facing page bottom: hopefuls panning for gold and (above) an old gold dredge, a machine designed to do the job faster, both around Fairbanks. Top: a satellite tracking station run by NASA at Gilmore Creek near Fairbanks, and (overleaf) nearby forest.

Sadly, in some parts of the United States, such an orange tinge to river water could be an indication of pollution. Here, in Denali National Park (left and overleaf), it is merely the color of the park's soil – the water is as pure as nature allows. In these 9,000 square miles north of Anchorage, everything possible is done to ensure the park remains unblemished by humanity, even to the extent of limiting the numbers of private cars that drive through the park. Visitors are required to leave their vehicles at the park entrance and take a ranger-driven "Wilderness Bus" into Denali's interior, a policy designed to reduce man's disturbance of an area spectacularly rich in wildlife.

To see Mount McKinley (these pages) is to appreciate why the Alaskan Indians called the mountain Denali – "The Great One." This is one of the world's great mountains, not only for its height but also for its setting: when McKinley lets fall its veil of mist, the eye is given an uninterrupted sweep along its superb shoulders to the summit as no other mountain in the immediate vicinity comes near to challenging this peak. Particularly good views are to be had from the Susitna River (above) and the George Parks Highway (left), which skirts Denali National Park.

Born beside the seemingly unyielding granite shoulders of Mount McKinley, the Ruth Glacier (right and overleaf) flows smoothly down the lesser peaks of the Alaskan Range, one of at least a dozen major glaciers spawned in the part of the range within Denali National Park. Considering the high elevation, the low oxygen levels and the extreme cold, the feat of two miners, Billy Taylor and Pete Anderson — the first people to scale the North Peak of McKinley, in 1910 — was quite incredible. Until this attempt they had never climbed any mountain, yet, undaunted, they sallied forth with a thermos of hot chocolate, a bag of doughnuts for their lunch and a spruce flagpole from which to fly "Old Glory" at the "summit." Setting off from 11,000 feet, they climbed the final 10,000 feet in a day, returning with two doughnuts to spare. Their inexperience probably accounted for their crucial mistake, though — the North Peak is 850 feet lower than the South Peak, so, sadly, these intrepid amateurs failed to reach the true summit.

The evening light outlining the velvet on their new growth of antlers, a pair of caribou pause to test the air. Both sexes grow antlers, but cast them before the winter, as the weight would be an unnecessary load to bear during severe weather. A walking caribou makes a characteristic clicking sound due to the action of its sinews – a sound that accompanies it all its waking life, since it is forever on the move, stopping only to mate or give birth. This continual movement is demanded by the limitations of the tundra as pasture: should the animals overgraze one area, tiny plants such as reindeer moss, upon which caribou rely, would soon be destroyed.

Right: looking like bottle brushes, ranks of evergreens stand stiffly in the snow in Denali National Park (overleaf), where a gold tinge to the tundra indicates that the park's brief autumn has begun. This starts in late August, when a fine tapestry of reds and russets spreads across the park for a few short weeks prior to the first winter blizzards. The first white man to explore the Denali region extensively was Charles Sheldon, a member of the powerful Boone and Crockett Club. Particularly impressed with the abundant wildlife he found here, and anxious to preserve it, Sheldon began to use his influence to muster support for the formation of a national park and, largely due to his efforts, his dream became a reality in 1917. However, it was only upon completion of the Anchorage-Fairbanks Highway in 1972 that the beauties of Denali came to the attention of the general public, as only then was the region easily accessible.

Named for the safe harbor it offers, Anchorage started as a railroad tent camp in 1913, a busy construction base for the nation's first federally built and operated railroad. Today it is the largest city in the state, Alaska's premier port and her commercial and financial center. During the oil boom of the early Eighties, half the state's residents lived here – a population of 250,000 with a median age of twenty-eight. Since then, over 20,000 people have moved away, but those that remain enjoy the third highest per capita income in the United States – and, perhaps surprisingly, the country's highest per capita consumption of ice cream!

Not only do most of the state's roads converge on Anchorage (these pages), but its international airport is a world air crossroads, a fact proudly recorded on an impressive city signpost (facing page). The airport welcomes three million travelers a year, many of them famous – once, as their paths crossed between their separate flights, President Ronald Reagan and Pope John Paul II exchanged words in the departure lounge here.

Protected from the most severe weather by the Chugach and Kenai mountains to the east and the Alaskan Range to the north, Anchorage (these pages) sparkles in spring sunshine while it could be raining – or even snowing – on the other side of the mountains. Nevertheless, the city's location does have some disadvantages. The Alaskan Range contains active volcanoes, one of which erupted as recently as 1976, covering the city with a fine layer of ash, while in 1964 the most powerful earthquake ever recorded on the North American continent devastated many Anchorage homes and businesses. Most city dwellers, however, consider their new combination of condominiums and log cabins a fine balance between the wilderness around them and the advantages of modern life.

"The Last Great Race," the Iditarod Trail Sled Dog Race (these pages and overleaf), is run each year from Anchorage to Nome on a route over 1,000 miles in length. In honor of the occasion, the whole state rouses itself to follow the contestants' every move. One of the reasons the race appeals to spectators is that rank outsiders often walk away with the laurels. A dog musher may use the finest equipment, the best-bred huskies and have meticulously planned the optimum places for trail drops of supplies, but success in the Iditarod is never a foregone conclusion – luck plays a crucial part, as any winner would concede. Even finishing is a great achievement, as to do so means racing through blizzards, freezing temperatures and blinding winds. In the end, strong-hearted huskies are as important as swift ones, and courage and determination are common virtues among Iditarod mushers.

Between them, Lake Hood (above) and Lake Spenard, adjacent to Alaska International Airport in Anchorage, are the home of the world's largest base for float planes, the tiny aircraft upon which many Interior communities rely for their supplies and transport. Not surprisingly, more people have pilot licenses in Alaska than in any other state. Above right and right: the waters of Turnagain Arm to the south of Anchorage, named for the U-turn the English explorer Captain Cook was obliged to make when he realised that this was a dead end rather than the longed-for Northwest Passage.

Equipped with waders, plastic buckets and long-handled nets, fishermen try their luck for smelt in Turnagain Arm. Known as dip-netters, these men and women have to take great care to select a safe area of mudflat not far from the rocks of the shore. Turnagain Arm is notoriously dangerous, as the incoming tides cause the mudflats to act like quicksand. Also, the arm is regularly swept by a great tidal bore, whose speed can take walkers on the mud by surprise. So fast does the water wall approach that even helicopters – the quickest means of rescue available – have failed to reach stranded walkers before the tide engulfed them. Overleaf: the yacht harbor at Seward, a port south of Anchorage on the Gulf of Alaska.

Above and left: ice-cold Portage Creek, which flows into Turnagain Arm (overleaf) from Portage Glacier, one of southcentral Alaska's most popular tourist destinations. Portage Glacier recreation area, maintained by the Forest Service, provides viewing telescopes and information about the glacier, and gold panning and nature walks are organized to entertain visitors. Once, the eastern end of Turnagain Arm was headed by the town of Portage, but today only ruins remain, as the town was destroyed during the 1964 earthquake. The countryside (above left) around the former town, however, remains as coolly serene as ever.

Seward (these pages), snuggling at the foot of the Chugach Mountains, is a favorite vacation center for sports fisherman. Thousands come to the town each August for the Silver Salmon Derby, eight-and-a-half days of round-the-clock fishing where the successful can net prizes totalling $45,000. Though it is one of the main occupations, fishing isn't all that takes place at Seward. Equally popular is the Mount Marathon Race, held in July, in which runners race to the top of a nearby 3,022-foot-high peak and slither down again. The record time for the run, which began as a wager between two sourdoughs in 1909, is a mere forty-three minutes.

The serene waters of Aialik Bay wash the feet of the Kenai Mountains as they meet the sea near Seward. Reaching over 6,500 feet in height, these peaks surround the huge Harding Icefield, allowing only narrow channels for the glaciers it engenders to slink through down to the dark water. Ice compacts to form three major glaciers in this bay, each incised by Arctic winds and all dissolving in a salty sea.

These pages: tidewater glaciers sprawl into Aialik Bay. The Harding Icefield, which spawns these great ice rivers, is one of the largest in the world, spreading for 850 square miles across the Kenai Mountains on the Kenai Peninsula in southern Alaska. The concentrations of crevasses visible in some places on these glaciers are indications that the ice beneath is undergoing some stress, probably riding over a hill or into a "fall" below. Although a high peak across its path could deflect a glacier, there is no object on earth that would permanently prevent its slide down a mountain.

An orange windsock and scarlet fishnet floats brighten a wintery landscape of whites and greys in Homer, the southern terminus of the Sterling Highway on Kachemak Bay. Kachemak is an Aleutian word for "Smoky Bay," a name probably derived from the smoldering coal seams which were once visible along the bay's shore. The erosion of these bluffs creates a plentiful supply of winter fuel for Homer residents. The town lies near the Kenai Mountains, whose dramatic, sharp-toothed summits are some of the most beautiful in Alaska. Predictably, considering its scenery, Homer is a Mecca for artists, and a variety of galleries and studios flourish here and in the surrounding countryside.

Above: a fine catch of halibut (left) is hauled into the back of a pick-up truck in Homer harbor (above left). The waters of Kachemak Bay regularly yield rich harvests of this flat fish, plus salmon and king crab – indeed, halibut fishing trips are very popular with visitors to the bay, which is known throughout the state for the variety of its marine life. A boat can be hired from the local marina (overleaf), and whales, sea otters, puffins, seals and porpoises are all regularly sighted on such fishing trips.

At Eklutna, a tiny village of some thirty or so Indians lying just northeast of Anchorage, Alaskan Indian spirit houses (these pages) protect the treasured possessions of departed souls beside a log-built Siberian prayer chapel and a Russian Orthodox Church. The spirit houses in this cemetery are painted in the traditional colors of the families to which they belong; Eastern Orthodox crosses placed beside them indicate the Indians' later conversion to Orthodox Christianity. Overleaf: enormous moose antlers decorate a pole beside Nikolai's cheerful welcome sign on the Iditarod Trail to Nome.

A plump ginger tom warily crosses a dirt street
bedecked with telegraph wire in Nome, the state's
dog-mushing capital, on the Alaskan east coast.
In March, the Month of the Iditarod, a festival
celebrating the famed 1,049-mile-long Iditarod
Dog Sled Race, which ends in Nome, is held here.
In reality the race is closer to 1,200 miles in
length – 1,049 was picked as the traditional
distance because Alaska is the forty-ninth state.
Nome was in existence by the end of 1900, since
some 20,000 people had flooded the area that year
after a gold strike was made on Nome beach. The
sands were turned over dozens of times and
yielded millions of dollars in gold. Nome's
population today is just under 3,500, but it is
still possible to pan for gold on this famous beach,
and what is found belongs to whoever panned it –
just like in the old days. It can be worth the effort
– a gold nugget weighing an ounce was
discovered here under driftwood in 1984.

Above: vigilant huskies guard the bleached driftwood and rusting metal that comprises just some of the flotsam surrounding an Inuit's corrugated-iron house in Nome. Although it is externally drab and ramshackle, it is likely that the interior of this home will glow with warmth and color. Here, freight rates are high and building materials are scarce, so driftwood and salvage are in common usage for house construction. Above left: fishing equipment on Nome beach and (left) dried grass, the only "gold" remaining around an old gold dredger on a Nome river.

Smooth and modern, the parabola of a
telecommunications dish fronts the storm-torn
winter shoreline of Nome. On some parts of this
coast the winter winds are so strong that the
inhabitiants are obliged to crawl along the
ground in order to avoid being blown over.
Mindful of such conditions, a huge sea wall of
boulders has been built alongside Nome's Front
Street, a road which lies right at the water's edge,
to protect the town from the furious storms that
blow in from the Bering Sea. In 1974, the town
was all but devastated when such a storm
overcame the sea wall and engulfed most of the
buildings on the shore side of Front Street. The
following morning Nome looked as if it had
suffered a mortar attack, but its intrepid citizens
soon reconstructed it within a strongly
reinforced sea wall.

Above left: chained apart in a line to thwart their tendency to fight one another, a husky team on Nome beach begins to give voice in warning as the photographer approaches. Left: looking like giant fillets of frozen fish, ice starts to break up on the Nome River (above) beside an outlying settlement of Nome, where the floes and water echo the clouds and sky of a spring day. Mindful of the practical uses of their surroundings, the Inuit of Nome, and elsewhere in western Alaska, still store seal meat, walrus, fish and caribou steaks in natural deep freezes dug out of the permafrost, but these days they may consider a cache of T.V. dinners too – and apparently they do also buy refrigerators!

Facing page: (top) a grisly collection of skulls and antlers on a Kotzebue roof and, nearby, salmon (bottom) draped over a pole to dry. Kotzebue (these pages) began as a reindeer station, and this remains a significant part of the town's economy. Despite the rigors of life within the Arctic Circle, this town has a sense of humor. Those sent to find Kotzebue National Forest will discover an imported and cherished lone spruce – as the only tree for a hundred miles, the residents are very proud of it.

Serving as the midnight sun in midwinter
Alaska, a perfect full moon shines on a husky
team in a lunar Arctic landscape. The Siberian
husky is the oldest breed of sled dog used in
Alaska, and its role in Arctic transportation and
exploration has been incalculable. As a sled dog
of strength and stamina, in severe weather a fine
Siberian husky can be worth its weight in gold.
Overleaf: snow blown into wave-like formations
on the frozen Bering Sea. Such intense cold does
eventually concede to the long-awaited spring
sunshine (following page).